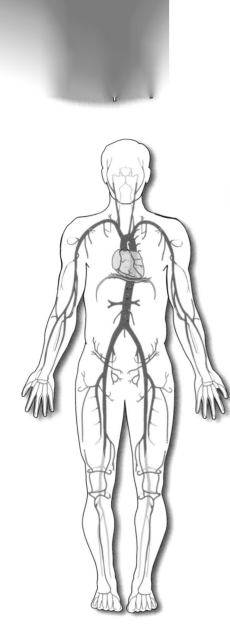

Heart Man

Vivien Thomas, African-American Heart Surgery Pioneer

Edwin Brit Wyckoff

Enslow Elementary

an imprint of

Enslow Publishers, Inc.

40 Industrial Road
Box 398
Berkeley Heights, NJ 07922
USA

http://www.enslow.com

Series Literacy Consultant

Allan A. De Fina, Ph.D.
Past President of the New Jersey Reading Association
Professor, Department of Literacy Education
New Jersey City University

Enslow Elementary, an imprint of Enslow Publishers, Inc.

Enslow Elementary® is a registered trademark of Enslow Publishers, Inc.

Library of Congress Cataloging-in-Publication Data

Wyckoff, Edwin Brit.
    Heart man : Vivien Thomas, African-American heart surgery pioneer / by Edwin Brit Wyckoff.
        p. cm. — (Genius at work! Great inventor biographies)
    Includes bibliographical references and index.
    Summary: "Biography of Vivien Thomas, the mastermind behind open-heart surgery"—Provided by publisher.
    ISBN-13: 978-0-7660-2849-4
    ISBN-10: 0-7660-2849-6
        1. Thomas, Vivien T., 1910–1985—Juvenile literature. 2. Surgeons—Maryland—Biography—
Juvenile literature. 3. Cardiovascular system—Surgery—Juvenile literature. I. Title.
    RD27.35.T46W93 2007
    617.008996073—dc22
    [B]
                                                    2006100567

Printed in the United States of America

10 9 8 7 6 5 4 3 2

To Our Readers

We have done our best to make sure all Internet addresses in this book were active and appropriate when we went to press. However, the author and the publisher have no control over and assume no liability for the material available on those Internet sites or on other Web sites they may link to. Any comments or suggestions can be sent by e-mail to comments@enslow.com or to the address on the back cover.

Every effort has been made to locate all copyright holders of material used in this book. If any errors or omissions have occurred, corrections will be made in future editions of this book.

Photo Credits: Courtesy of The Alan Mason Chesney Medical Archives of The Johns Hopkins Medical Institutions, pp. 3 (inset), 11, 16, 18, 20, 21, 24; *Alfred Blalock* by Isabella Hunner Parsons, oil on canvas, courtesy of The Alan Mason Chesney Medical Archives of The Johns Hopkins Medical Institutions, photo by Aaron Levin, p. 27 (right); *Anna* by De Nyselo Turner, oil on canvas, courtesy of The Alan Mason Chesney Medical Archives of The Johns Hopkins Medical Institutions, photo by Aaron Levin, p. 28; © CORBIS, p. 23 (article photo); Herbert Hoover Presidential Library, image 1930-76B, p. 10; Historical Collection, Eskind Biomedical Library, Vanderbilt University Medical Center, Nashville, TN, p. 12; © 2007 Jupiterimages Corporation, Inc., p. 7 (all except bottom left); Life Art image copyright 1998 Lippincott Williams & Wilkins. All rights reserved, pp. 1 (left), 3 (background), 17, 22 (both); Courtesy of the Martin Photo Collection at the Iberia Parish Library in New Iberia, image 10,756, p. 6; Shutterstock, p. 7 (bottom left); Copyright © 1946. The New York Times Co. Reprinted by permission, p. 23 (article text); Courtesy of Thomas Family/Spark Media, pp. 1 (right), 4, 8, 14; *Vivien Thomas* by Bob Gee, oil on canvas, courtesy of The Alan Mason Chesney Medical Archives of The Johns Hopkins Medical Institutions, photo by Aaron Levin, p. 27 (left); Courtesy of the Vivien Thomas Family, p. 13.

Front Cover: Shutterstock (background); *Vivien Thomas* by Bob Gee, oil on canvas, courtesy of The Alan Mason Chesney Medical Archives of The Johns Hopkins Medical Institutions, photo by Aaron Levin (inset)

Back Cover: Shutterstock

Contents

Vivien Thomas

Chapter 1

Where Is Vivien?

The room was as dark as night. A door opened. A nurse walked into the darkness. She turned on powerful lights in the operating room. Everything became bright as sunshine. A dozen doctors, nurses, and medical technicians poured into the super-clean room at Johns Hopkins Hospital in Baltimore, Maryland. They checked every medical tool. Nobody talked, because this day was not like any other day. This highly trained team was going to operate on a baby's heart to try to save its life. It was November 29, 1944. The operation had never been done on a person before.

The surgeon, Dr. Alfred Blalock, held out his hand for a very sharp scalpel. He raised it over the baby's chest. Then he stopped and shouted, "Where is Vivien? Go get him."

The man whom Dr. Blalock needed in that operating room was a thirty-four-year-old black researcher named Vivien Theodore Thomas. He was not a medical doctor, and he never would be.

Vivien was born on August 29, 1910, in New Iberia, Louisiana. His father, William, was a successful carpenter. Before Vivien, the family

New Iberia, Louisiana, 1910

already had three boys. Mary, his mother, was so sure her next child would be a girl that she named it Vivian before it was born. When boy number four arrived, she kept the name, but changed it to Vivien to make it into a boy's name.

Carpenter's tools

In 1912, William and Mary Thomas moved their family to Nashville, a big city in Tennessee. William and his older sons built a comfortable house for the family.

Later on, the teenage Vivien also became a very good carpenter. His father expected Vivien to work with him full time after finishing high school. Vivien had other ideas. His mind was set on becoming

Pearl High School was the only high school for African Americans in North Nashville. Vivien graduated with honors.

a doctor. That was a very big dream for an African American in those days.

Learning carpentry had taught Vivien how to be careful. He always measured twice so that he would have to cut just once. He never wasted wood, and he never wasted time. Even as a teenager, Vivien began earning good money and started saving for medical school. He graduated with honors from Pearl High School in 1929. He could see his future as a doctor.

Chapter

The Dream Becomes a Nightmare

The year 1930 changed Vivien Thomas's life. The country was slowing down during the terrible times of the Great Depression. Companies around the country had lost money in the stock market crash. Many people lost their jobs. Banks went out of business. Thomas's bank slammed its doors shut. The bank had lost every dollar Thomas had saved for medical school.

Thomas was out of school and out of work. Then one day a friend took him to meet Dr. Alfred Blalock at Vanderbilt University Medical School in Nashville. The famous and powerful doctor hired him as an assistant in his medical research laboratory.

This photo shows the New York Stock Exchange just after the stock market crashed in October, 1929. This marked the beginning of the Great Depression.

Step by step, the doctor began to trust Thomas with simple research work. Dr. Blalock was impressed with Thomas's skills. The doctor was a great teacher who was always willing to take time to answer questions. But Dr. Blalock had another side that Thomas discovered soon enough.

One day, Thomas heard an explosion of words. Dr. Blalock was ranting, raving, and running around, knocking down tools. He was screaming out swear words and shouting that nobody ever did anything right. The doctor thought that Thomas had not kept perfect records of their experiments. He was wild with anger at Thomas.

With great sadness, Thomas knocked on Dr. Blalock's office door and asked for his pay. He could not work for a doctor who yelled at him like a crazy man. For Thomas it was a

Dr. Alfred Blalock gave Thomas a job in his research laboratory.

matter of self-respect. He did not complain or explain. He just wanted to leave.

Most of Dr. Blalock's workers suffered through his wild outbursts without saying anything. They would rather risk their pride than risk their job. But Thomas would not stand for it. He walked out.

The brilliant and powerful doctor, who at that time was a famous star of surgery, ran after Thomas and apologized. He promised he would never yell at him again. He kept that promise.

Thomas did many experiments in Dr. Blalock's medical research laboratory.

Dr. Blalock and Vivien Thomas were two very different kinds of men, but they shared a love of medical research. Both worked long hours at the hospital without complaining.

Thomas spent his nights and weekends building a house in Nashville with his own hands. He met a lovely young woman named Clara Beatrice Flanders

Clara Beatrice Flanders married Thomas in December 1933. The next year, their first daughter was born.

and married her on December 22, 1933. Their first girl, Olga Fay, was born the next year. Another girl, Theodosia Patricia, was born four years later.

Thomas with his family, shortly before the move to Baltimore.

Chapter 3

Partners of the Heart

Whenever Thomas asked Dr. Blalock to ask the medical school for a pay raise, the doctor delayed and delayed. Thomas deserved a raise. He was doing difficult experiments. He had learned how to do surgery on laboratory animals. But he faced an endless struggle to support his family on the same low pay a janitor earned. Once more, Thomas told Dr. Blalock that he was being forced to quit. Finally, the doctor got the school to give him a raise. It was not much more money, but it helped.

In 1940, Dr. Blalock accepted a very important position as head of surgery at the world-famous Johns Hopkins Hospital in Baltimore, Maryland. He asked Thomas to come along as part of his team.

Clara and the children moved with him to Baltimore in July of 1941.

The new neighborhood was run down. Thomas's pay was still so low he had to take extra jobs as a bartender to pay his bills. He did not want to leave the hospital, though, because the work he was doing there was so interesting. Medical research had become his life.

Dr. Helen Taussig hoped Thomas and Dr. Blalock could find a way to help blue babies.

Thomas's world changed again when he and Dr. Blalock met Dr. Helen Taussig, a heart doctor for children, in 1943. She showed them "blue babies." They were so sick that most did not live very long. Dr. Taussig knew that surgery had never been planned on a human heart.

Still, she asked Dr. Blalock and Thomas to find a way to use surgery to keep these children alive.

Other doctors warned Dr. Blalock, Dr. Taussig, and Thomas that nobody should operate on someone's beating heart. This was a basic rule of medicine that those doctors said should not be broken.

But Dr. Blalock and Thomas did not listen. They studied the problem for months. They figured out a way to repair the heart. It would be very dangerous.

What Is a Blue Baby?

FACT

A blue baby is a child born with a heart that does not work properly. The heart does not pump enough blood from the lungs. As a result, the blood does not have enough oxygen. Blood that lacks oxygen is blue, so their lips, eyelids, fingernails, and toes are blue instead of pink. It hurts them to breathe. When they are old enough to go out and play, even a few slow steps seem to wear them out. Much of the time, these young children sit quietly in bed with their arms folded around their knees. That seems to help them breathe with less pain.

Thomas needed to know that operating on a blue baby's heart was safe. So he practiced the heart surgery on laboratory dogs. He gave the dogs medicine so they would not feel pain. Most times, he worked alone.

Each operation failed, but each one taught him a new way to operate or the need for a new tool. He made new tools that could cut and sew in very tiny spaces.

After almost two hundred operations, Thomas, the quiet, careful scientist, operated on a dog named Anna. This time the little dog survived. Blood poured through her lungs, giving her the oxygen her body needed. Thomas's cutting and stitching were so perfect that Dr. Blalock said they seemed to be "something that the Lord made."

Operating on a heart is very difficult because there is very little room to work. Thomas invented this clamp to help stop bleeding in a very small space.

Chapter 4

To Save a Life

Eileen Saxon was fifteen months old. She weighed only nine pounds. Her lips were blue. Her face had a soft blue color. Eileen's heart did not pump blood into her lungs the way it should. She would be the first patient.

Dr. Blalock was surrounded by nurses ready to hand him instruments. Assistants waited with sponges to clear away blood. Dr. Blalock barked out the order to get Vivien Thomas. Nurses ran through the research laboratories looking for him. They found Thomas working in the laboratory as though it were just an ordinary day. It was not.

Thomas raced to the operating room, washed up, and put on surgical gloves and a mask.

Dr. Blalock pointed to a wooden stool right behind his elbow. He wanted Thomas to stand on it so that he could see over the doctor's shoulder. Step by step, Thomas and the doctor talked back and forth throughout the operation. The first artery was cut. The clamps Thomas had created stopped the bleeding.

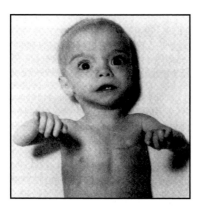

After the surgery, the scar from the operation can be seen on Eileen Saxon's chest.

The two men became a fantastic operating team. One was the chief surgeon at a famous hospital. The other was a thirty-four-year-old black researcher—he was not a doctor at all.

Dr. Blalock used one finger to reach into Eileen's tiny body. He stitched the artery so that it fed blood directly to her lungs. Thomas and Dr. Blalock whispered words so softly the others could hardly hear them. The surgeon sewed the artery in place. After three hours, the operation was over.

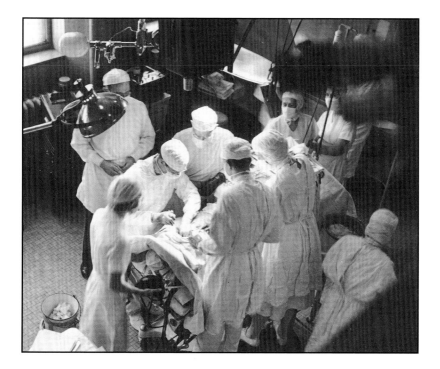

Dr. Blalock is seen here operating on a blue baby. Vivien Thomas stands right behind him.

They had saved a child so small that the baby's arm was only a bit larger than the doctor's index finger. Vivien Thomas stepped down from the stool and went back to his work in the laboratory. Dr. Blalock and the others glowed with excitement. Not one of them would ever forget that day. During the next two weeks, Eileen turned from blue to healthy pink. It was marvelous.

Dr. Blalock and Thomas decided to operate on the heart of a blue baby. They would need to cut and move one of the arteries. They would sew the artery to a blood vessel that would send the blood directly to the lungs. This would repair the heart.

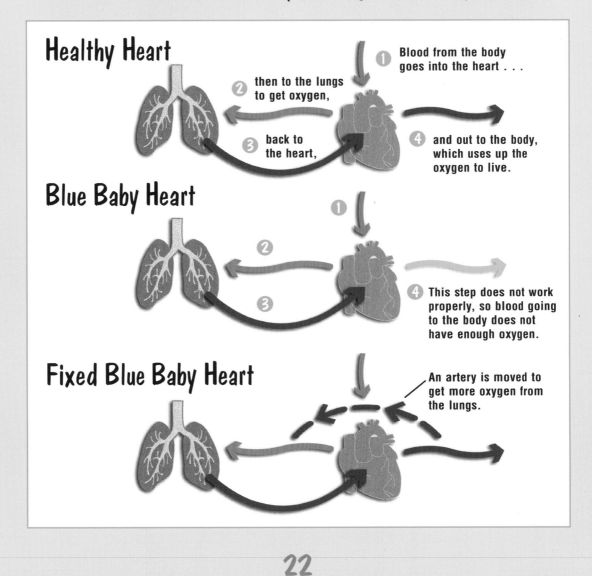

Healthy Heart

1 Blood from the body goes into the heart . . .

2 then to the lungs to get oxygen,

3 back to the heart,

4 and out to the body, which uses up the oxygen to live.

Blue Baby Heart

1

2

3

4 This step does not work properly, so blood going to the body does not have enough oxygen.

Fixed Blue Baby Heart

An artery is moved to get more oxygen from the lungs.

News of the "blue baby" operations flashed around the world. Parents came cradling blue babies in their arms, begging for help. Thomas assisted Dr. Blalock on the first hundred operations. Magazines and newspapers rushed to Johns Hopkins Hospital to take pictures of everyone on the medical team. But one man's face was always missing from the photos.

How 2 Doctors Give New Lives To Blue Babies

Blalock-Taussig Operation, First Tested on Dogs, Reroutes Flow of Blood

By Lester Grant

BALTIMORE, Feb. 14.—This is the story of the work of two doctors—a man from Georgia and a woman from Massachusetts—who met in Baltimore and combined their talents to save the lives of "blue babies."

The doctors are Alfred Blalock, forty-six, surgeon in chief at Johns Hopkins Hospital here and professor of surgery at the Hopkins Medical School, and Helen B. Taussig, forty-seven, physician in charge of the cardiac clinic of the Harriet Lane Home for Invalid Children. The Harriet Lane Home constitutes the pediatrics division of Johns Hopkins Hospital.

The surgery, known as the Blalock-Taussig operation, first was used on an infant on Nov. 29, 1944. Its development since then is one of the most exciting stories in

Dr. Alfred Blalock and Dr. Helen B. Taussig at Johns Hopkins Hospital in Baltimore

Newspaper articles, like this one from the *New York Herald Tribune*, talked about Dr. Blalock and Dr. Taussig, but left out Thomas.

Vivien Thomas surprised people when they saw him in a white lab coat. In the 1940s, African Americans were not expected to be doctors.

Chapter 5

The Invisible Black Man

The face of the missing man was black. The laboratory coat he wore was bright white. Vivien Thomas could still remember the first time he walked through the halls of a hospital wearing his white laboratory coat. People had turned to stare. Back then, an African-American man was expected to wear a janitor's uniform, not a white medical coat.

Dr. Blalock had worked one-on-one with Thomas for many years. He depended on Thomas's genius for surgery. But he would not invite him to a celebration party. The doctor could not overcome being raised to believe that one race was better than another. It took a long, long time for many Americans to see the person inside and not the color outside. It is still a problem in the United States today.

Dr. Denton Cooley had been on the team for the first "blue baby" operation. He described Thomas's work by saying, "There wasn't a false move, not a wasted motion when he operated." He remembered, "It was Vivien who had worked it all out in the laboratory, in a dog's heart long before Eileen. . . . There were no heart experts then. That was the beginning." That beginning changed the world of heart surgery. Since then, millions of heart operations have been done, not just on children, but on people of all ages.

Dr. Blalock died in 1964. Vivien Thomas was fifty-four years old then. He would go on running the laboratory for fifteen more years. The man who could not afford medical school later trained hundreds of surgeons.

Johns Hopkins University made Thomas an Honorary Doctor of Laws in 1976. Although he had been teaching medical students for years, he was officially appointed as an instructor of surgery. His portrait was painted and placed in

These portraits of Thomas and Dr. Blalock hang at Johns Hopkins Hospital today.

the same hall at Johns Hopkins Hospital as that of Dr. Blalock. The two geniuses will be remembered for generations to come. Vivien Thomas died in Baltimore on November 26, 1985.

Also in the halls of the hospital hangs a portrait of the dog Anna. She was Thomas's first successful patient for the "blue baby" operation. Vivien Thomas, the carpenter who became a scientist, had proved to the world that surgery on a beating heart can be done safely.

When Anna survived the operation, Thomas knew that his work would be able to help blue babies.

1910 Born on August 29 in New Iberia, Louisiana.

1912 Moves with family to Nashville, Tennessee.

1929 Graduates from Pearl High School with honors.

1930 Loses all his savings when Peoples Bank closes its doors; starts work as a laboratory technician for Dr. Alfred Blalock at Vanderbilt University School of Medicine.

1933 Marries Clara Beatrice Flanders on December 22, with whom he will have two daughters.

1941 Follows Dr. Blalock to Johns Hopkins Hospital in Baltimore, Maryland.

1944 Advises Dr. Blalock step by step through the first blue baby operation, November 29, which is successful.

1964 Continues researching and teaching surgery after Dr. Blalock dies, September 15.

1976 Is awarded an honorary degree by Johns Hopkins University and is officially appointed an instructor in surgery, even though he is not a medical doctor.

1979 Retires from hospital work.

1985 Dies of natural causes on November 26.

artery—A large blood vessel that leads out of the heart. It carries blood to all the smaller blood vessels.

blood vessel—One of the tubes that carries blood from the heart to the lungs, back to the heart, and then around to all the parts of the body.

experiment—A very carefully planned test of something that has not been tried before.

medical research—The study of how to help people stay well or get well when they are sick.

medical technician—Someone who is trained to use special tools to help doctors work on patients.

operating room—A special spick-and-span room in a hospital with bright lights and all the tools needed for surgery.

oxygen—A part of the air we breathe that is needed for people and animals to live.

scalpel—A surgeon's knife.

surgeon—A doctor who is specially trained to cut into patients to help cure them.

Books

Curry, Don L. *How Does Your Heart Work?* Conn.: Children's Press, 2004.

Curry, Don L. *How Do Your Lungs Work?* Conn.: Children's Press, 2004.

Stewart, Gail B. *Racism*. San Diego, Calif.: KidHaven Press, 2002.

Internet Addresses

Let's Learn About Your Heart!
http://www.mplsheart.org/kids/

All About the Heart
http://kidshealth.org/kid/htbw/heart.html

Index